ESSAYS

ON

THE BOOK OF PROVERBS.

BY

(a.) S. SEKLES,
(b.) GRANVILLE ROSS PIKE.

PHILADELPHIA:

Published by the Young Men's Hebrew
Association.

1888.

In the interest of creating a more extensive selection of rare historical book reprints, we have chosen to reproduce this title even though it may possibly have occasional imperfections such as missing and blurred pages, missing text, poor pictures, markings, dark backgrounds and other reproduction issues beyond our control. Because this work is culturally important, we have made it available as a part of our commitment to protecting, preserving and promoting the world's literature. Thank you for your understanding.

PREFACE.

In the summer of 1886 the Board of Managers of the Young Men's Hebrew Association of Philadelphia, desiring to encourage the study of Hebrew Literature, issued the following circular, which was widely distributed in such quarters from which it was thought a response might be elicited:

The Young Men's Hebrew Association of Philadelphia offers a Prize of Fifty (50) Dollars for the best Essay submitted on the following topic:

The Principles of Ethics in the Sayings Contained in the Book of Proverbs, with an Inquiry into the Social Conditions which They Reflect.

The judges of the Essays will be:

> Dr. M. Jastrow, Philadelphia.
> Dr. G. Gottheil, New York.
> Dr. B. Felsenthal, Chicago.

The Committee has adopted the following rules:

1. The competition is open to all.

2. Every Essay submitted must be written in English, and must be originally prepared for this competition.

3. Essays must be written on one side of the paper only.

4. Essays must be sent to Dr. M. Jastrow, 925 North Eighth Street, Philadelphia, on or before April 1, 1887.

5. Each Essay must be signed with an assumed name. A sealed envelope endorsed with the assumed name, and containing the true name of the writer, must accompany the Essay.

6. The successful Essay shall become the property of the Association, which may, in its discretion and at its own expense, publish the same.

A number of Essays were submitted to the judges, who, after a careful consideration, reported to the Board of Managers of the Association that in their judgment the Essay of Mr. S. Sekles, of New York, was entitled to the prize, and recommended that honorable mention be made of the Essay of the Rev. Granville Ross Pike, of Clayville, New York. The report of the judges having been confirmed by the Board, the award was duly made in accordance therewith.

The Ethics of Mishle.

BY S. SEKLES.

A book highly praised but little read, greatly esteemed but little known, is *Mishle*, the Book of Proverbs, one of the Holy Scriptures. It is a collection of works of several writers, most, if not all, of whom lived during the First Hebrew Commonwealth, and has for its main purpose the manners and proprieties, the rules and requirements of social and practical life. The Book of Proverbs was always looked upon with great favor, and was highly esteemed by our ancient Rabbis. They saw in proverbs a main support of the precepts of the *Torah*. "Do not despise the *Mashal* (proverb), for it contributes to the understanding of the *Torah*" (*Midrash Rabbah* to *Shir Hashirim*). They illustrated this assertion by numerous similes, among others, by comparing the proverb to a candle, which, though of insignificant value, may be the means whereby a great treasure may be discovered. One of the greatest thinkers of the second century, Bar Kappora, even asserted, that one sentence of *Mishle*, namely, "In all thy ways acknowledge God, and He shall direct thy paths" (III. 6), comprises the very essence of the laws of the *Torah* (*B'reshith Rabbah*, section 63). The different authors seem to have written exclusively for that large body of the people who formed the middle classes, the farmer, the mechanic, and the small merchant, while they rarely addressed the judges, the wealthy, and never the priests or government officers. They occupied themselves more with the life of the individual than that of the community, so that it should become a family book, a *Vade mecum* for the house. This peculiar feature of *Mishle* manifests a prominent trait of the Jewish spirit in contradistinction to the entire literature of the ancient world. Among other nations the individual received consideration only as a part of the political body. The totality alone was thought worthy of account and report; the individual disappeared. The Hebrews, on the other hand, devoted careful consideration to the individual and the family life.

We can only notice here that this characteristic contributed to the salvation of the people, when their state and their religious institutions were destroyed.

The compilers of *Mishle* avoided all metaphysical investigations and speculations, and did not indulge in abstract problems, but when they accidentally touched them, expressed their views in short, concise sentences.

They sought to deduce from the thoughts of other Biblical books, moral and religious principles which should be universal and applicable wherever man lived. Though sacrifice, for example, is alluded to once or twice, no importance is attached to the ritual system. The ideas around which prophecy revolves, such as the kingdom of God, of a chosen people, of a Messiah, and the like, are entirely absent. The distinction between "Israel" and the "nations" has no place.

It would be, however, too hasty a conclusion to suppose any antagonism between the compilers of *Mishle* and either the priests or prophets.

The proverbs are entirely within the circle of revealed religion, as is evident from the fact that all the ethical rules contained therein are in conformity with the Law, and moreover repeatedly refer to the Law. To the sacrifices they referred as follows:

Honor the Lord from thy earnings,
And with the first fruit of all thine increase. (iii. 9.)

A high appreciation of prophecy is expressed in the sentence,

Without vision the people perish,
And he that keepeth the Law, happy be he. (xxix. 18.)

Virtues, however, like courage, patriotism, self-sacrifice, and public spirit, which form the military type, and overshadowed all other sentiments in other nations, are not touched upon; only amiable traits, like benevolence, charity, love, reverence, which are closely connected with religion and a moral life, are prominently and impressively taught.

It was not until a later period than the time of the composition of *Mishle*, when formidable empires sprang up around Palestine, and the danger of destruction grew imminent, that military virtues became a necessity. When courage, patriotism, and self-sacrifice were needed for the preservation of independence, the Hebrews assumed these virtues, as is fully proved by history.

The leading idea of *Mishle* is, that the divine wisdom, grace, and love are the fundamental causes of all being. This is nowhere more strongly expressed than in the sublime speech which the ancient author puts in the mouth of eternal wisdom. (Ch. viii.)

"The true wisdom is the knowledge of the will of God," that is the recognition of the divine wisdom revealed in Nature and in the events of life. True wisdom includes all the spiritual and moral accomplishments of men, piety and skill, justice and discretion.

Of the attributes of God the proverbialists especially pronounce:

1. His omnipresence:

> The eyes of the Lord are in every place,
> Beholding the evil and the good.* (xv. 3.)

2. His omniscience:

Sheol and destruction are before the Lord,
How much more then the hearts of the children of men? (xv. 11.)

3. His providence:

> A man's heart deviseth his way,
> But the Lord directeth his steps. (xvi. 9.)

4. His infinite wisdom:

The Lord has with wisdom formed the earth,
And with understanding established the heavens. (iii. 19.)

5. His infinite justice:

Six things doth the Lord hate,
Seven are an abomination unto him.
A proud look, a lying tongue;
And hands that shed innocent blood;
A heart that deviseth wicked plans;
Feet that are swift in running to mischief;
A false witness speaking lies,
And he that soweth discord among brethren. (vi. 16-20.)

6. His infinite goodness:

> That thy trust may be in the Lord,
> I have made known to thee this day. (xxii. 19.)

The difficult problem how to reconcile the providence of God with the free will of man is not directly touched by our moralists. They accepted as an axiom that man is subject to the providence of God, but at the same time retains his free will.

---

* Rabbi Isaac Aboab makes the interesting remark that the verb *Tsaphah*, to behold, to penetrate with one's eyes, gives to this sentence the meaning that God understands the hypocrisy of persons, who deceive men, but whose thoughts are known to Him alone.

He that is slow to anger is better than the mighty,
And he that ruleth his spirit, than he that taketh a city.
(xvi. 32.)

Duties of Man.

As the main purpose of *Mishle* was to gather the most precious ethical doctrines of Israel, which appeal to man's reason and heart, we find there only such duties referred to as contribute directly to his justice, love, and moral purity, and are pre-eminently a matter of conscience.

The *fear of God* is repeatedly expressed as the highest principle of religion, in fact as religion itself. The Hebrew expression for fear of God, *Yirath Adonai*, does not mean as much apprehension of incurring God's wrath as the respectful reverence for His will, and the eager desire to fulfill His commands. Only in that sense could they say,

The fear of God is the beginning of knowledge (i. 7); it is the
fountain of life. (xiv. 27.)

Besides the fear of God our moralists pronounce trust in God as essential to a pure, moral life.

Thy trust may be in the Lord (xxii. 19);
He that putteth his trust in the Lord shall prosper. (xxviii. 25.)

The chief duty of man towards himself is beautifully and concisely expressed:

Keep thy heart with all diligence,
For out of it are the issues of life. (iv. 23.)

It is the heart with its emotions which requires rational control, and by directing it towards all that is good, noble, and pure, man secures perfection of mind and body.

In order to attain temporal happiness by perfecting and guarding a sound body, the following four virtues are urgently and repeatedly recommended: *temperance, contentment, industry,* and *chastity*.

The most beautiful admonitions against intemperance issued from one of our moralists:

Who hath woe? who hath sorrow?
Who hath contentions? who hath complaints?
Who hath wounds without cause?
Who hath his eyes darkened?
They that tarry long at the wine,
They that go to seek mixed wine.

> Be not tempted by the red wine,
> When it formeth pearls in the cup,
> And smoothly glideth down.
> At the last it biteth like a serpent,
> And stingeth like a viper. (xxiii. 29–32.)

Nevertheless our moralists did not oppose the moderate use of wine, and agreed with the Psalmists, "That wine cheers the heart of man," and recommend the drinking of it to cheer those in distress.

> Give strong wine unto him who is ready to perish,
> And wine to those that be of heavy heart.
> Let him drink and forget his sufferings,
> And remember his misery no more. (xxxi. 6–7.)

Our moralists fully appreciated that satisfaction of mind which is acquired by faith in God, and gives contentment to the soul.

> Better is little with the fear of the Lord,
> Than great treasure and troubles therewith. (xv. 16.)

The ancient Hebrews were an industrious people; labor was highly esteemed, and, therefore, repeatedly recommended:

> Go to the ant, thou sluggard,
> Consider her ways and be wise.
> She hath no guide, overseer, or ruler,
> Provideth her meat in summer,
> And gathereth her food in the harvest.
> How long wilt thou sleep, O sluggard?
> When wilt thou arise out of thy sleep?
> Yet a little sleep, a little slumber,
> A little folding of the hands to sleep,
> So shall thy poverty come as a traveler,
> And thy want as an armed man. (vi. 6–11.)

> The hand of the diligent shall bear rule,
> But the slothful shall be under tribute. (xii. 24.)

Love not sleep, lest thou come to poverty,
Open thine eyes and thou shalt be satisfied with bread. (xx. 13.)

The maxims in reference to the observance of chastity are among the most beautiful passages of the Holy Scriptures.

When man is in distress, suffering from the adversities of life, when misfortune pursues him, can better consolation and encouragement to *patience* and *hope* be found than in the following sayings?

My son, despise not the chastening of the Lord,
Neither be weary of his correction,
For whom the Lord loveth he correcteth,
Even as a father the son in whom he delighteth. (iii. 11-12.)

The proverbialists recommend *truthfulness, contentment*, and a cheerful disposition.

> Lying lips are abomination to the Lord,
> But they that deal truly are his delight. (xii. 22.)

> Better is little with the fear of the Lord,
> Than great treasure and trouble therewith. (xv. 16.)

> A merry heart giveth good health,
> But a broken spirit drieth the bones. (xvii. 22.)

While among other ancient nations such military virtues as courage, self-sacrifice, and patriotism secured to a citizen a lofty reputation, among the Hebrews it was piety, benevolence, and charity, which gave a man a *good name*, and our proverbialists recommended :

A good name rather is chosen than great riches,
And loving favor rather than silver and gold. (xxii. 1.)

If the Torah mentions in praise of the greatest man that ever lived, Moses, that he was meek, we may expect that meekness and modesty were especially appreciated and inculcated in the Proverbs.

Modesty was looked upon as the source of the fear of God, and the indirect cause of riches, honor, and happiness.

> In the wake of meekness are the fear of the Lord,
> Riches, honor and happiness. (xxii 4.)

On the contrary, *conceit* was repeatedly condemned, as for instance :

> Pride goes before destruction,
> And a haughty spirit before the fall. (xvi. 18.)

DUTIES TOWARDS OUR FELLOW-MEN.

The chief duties of man to his fellow-men are concisely and emphatically expressed in the Scriptural precept, "Thou shalt love thy neighbor as thyself." This precept implies positive and negative duties. The latter comprise prohibitions to injure our neighbor in his property, in reputation, or in peace of mind, and may be expressed as the *duty of justice*. The positive duties are those that have for their foundations *mercy*, and impel us to those amiable duties,—benevolence, sympathy, and charity.

These duties enjoined on us by the divine precept are beautifully expresssed by our moralists:

> He that pursueth righteousness and mercy,
> Findeth happiness, righteousness and honor. (xxi. 21.)

While this maxim comprises all our duties to our fellow-men, there are numerous others which refer to particular duties and especially to truthfulness and charity, of which we select:

> Withhold not good from them to whom it is due,
> When it is in thy power to do it.
> Say not unto thy neighbor, Go, and come again,
> And to-morrow I will give, when thou hast it by thee.
> Devise not evil against thy neighbor,
> Seeing he dwelleth securely by thee. (iii. 27-29.)
>
>> Strive not with a man without cause,
>> If he have done thee no harm. (iii. 30.)

> Whoso stoppeth his ears at the cry of the poor,
> He also shall cry himself, but shall not be heard. (xxi. 13.)

> He that oppresseth the poor reproacheth his Maker:
> But he that honoreth him hath mercy on the poor. (xiv. 31.)

A special characteristic of *Mishle* is shown in the recommendation concerning the treatment of enemies. This is another proof of the sublime ethical character prevailing among the Hebrews, inspired by their conceptions of God. Search the books of the ancient nations, decipher the inscriptions of the Assyrians and Babylonians for maxims like the following:

> If thine enemy be hungry give him bread to eat,
> And if he be thirsty, give him water to drink,
> For thou shalt heap coals of fire upon his head,
> And the Lord shall reward thee. (xxv. 21.)

> Rejoice not when thine enemy falleth,
> And let not thine heart be glad when he stumbleth. (xxiv. 17.)

In accordance with the general principles of morals are numerous maxims recommending prudence and discretion in social intercourse, all founded on the purest ethical basis.

It must be noticed that neither mixed marriages nor gambling are touched upon, an evident proof that they were unknown in the times of the authors of *Mishle*.

Social Conditions of the Hebrews.

While the prophets of Israel inveighed against the oppressions practised by the ruling powers and the corruption of the judges, the moralists of *Mishle* addressed themselves to the middle classes, and in their maxims and sayings reflect the social conditions of that large portion of the nation better than does any other part of the Bible.

Through the whole period of the first Commonwealth there existed a large class of farmers and tradesmen, who in the pursuit of their calling, although more or less affected by revolutions and wars, continued in the even tenor of their way, preserving the traditional ceremonies and customs, and keeping afar from the depraved influence of court life.

Out of the midst of the farmers the first prophet, the rustic and eloquent *Amos*, arose, whose speeches contain some of the most perfect specimens of sublime thought that are found in any language. He was only a herdsman, and his prophecies abound in illustrations drawn from husbandry and the scenes of rural life.

The people must have acquired a high degree of culture when such a man, a shepherd, could deliver such well set speeches, and could be understood and appreciated by his hearers.

We may assume that these patriots and God-inspired men, who composed or collected the most precious fruits of the wisdom of Israel, who were recognized under the pious king *Hezekiah*, as *the men of Hezekiah* (xxv. 1), and are mentioned by Isaiah as *my disciples* (Isaiah viii. 16), lived among the laboring classes, stood afar from the depraved influence of the ruling powers, and considered it their task to preserve the sacred spark of religion and pure morals among these classes, and to guard them from decline. Thanks to their efforts, the Hebrew farmer never sank down to the low grade of ignorant peasants of other countries, who, excluded from all education, were mere workers of the soil, standing not much higher than their domestic animals.

The land offered them inexhaustible sources of wealth. No part of Judea was waste, very little was occupied by unprofitable wood; the more fertile hills were cultivated in artificial terraces, others were adorned with orchards of fruit trees; the more rocky and barren districts were covered with vineyards. The climate was healthy and the seasons regular. Grain of all kinds—wheat, barley, millet, and other sorts—grew in abundance; the wheat commonly yielded thirty for one. Besides the wine and olive, the almond, the date, figs of many kinds, the orange, the pomegranate, and many other fruit trees flourished in the greatest luxuriance. Great quantities of honey were collected. Thus the farmer dwelt, according to the picturesque language of the country, each under his own vine or his own fig-tree, and could proudly say with the Shunammite, "I dwell among mine own people" (II. Kings iv. 13); I have no favors to ask from the king or his captains.

Besides the farmers there were many skilled mechanics in the country. There were *masons* (Masger) especially engaged in the erection of forts (II. Kings, xiv. 14), *sculptors* (Hosea xiii. 2), workers of mosaics, and of other trades. There were separate villages and districts occupied by the families of *Yokim*, of the tribe of Judah, engaged in manufacturing pottery, near Jerusalem (I. Chronicles iv. 22, 23). Not far from them lived the families of *Ashbia*, who wrought fine linen, a very fine tissue, hardly differing from our modern shirting.*

The wealth acquired by the diligence of the husbandman, by the industry of the skilled mechanic, and by the energy of the merchant, produced a certain opulence in all classes, that promoted a higher education and a general knowledge of reading and writing. The people were surrounded with a poetical, spiritual atmosphere. They listened to the fiery eloquence of the prophets, they sang the sublime poetry of the Psalmists, and recited the wise maxims of the moralists. Everything contributed towards raising them to a higher sphere.

Among such a nation the industrious were respected, and the slothful appeared despicable:

I went by the field of the slothful,
And by the vineyard of the man lacking understanding;
And lo, it was all grown with thorns,
And nettles covered the face thereof,
The stone wall thereof was broken down,
Then I saw and considered it well,
I looked upon it and received instruction.
Yet a little sleep, a little slumber,
A little folding of the hands to sleep,
So shall thy poverty come as a wayfarer,
And thy want as an armed man. (xxiv. 30, 34.)

Be thou diligent to know the condition of thy flocks,
And look well to thy herds.
The lambs are for thy clothing,
The young goats pay for the work on the field,

---

* According to an obscure passage in I. Kings x. 28, as translated by the Revised Version and explained by Kimchi, Solomon introduced the linen yarn from Egypt into Palestine.

Goats' milk will supply thy food and the food of thy household,
And maintenance for thy maidens.   (xxvii. 23, 26, 27.)

Mechanics also were encouraged to diligence :

Wealth gotten by vanity shall be diminished,
But he that gathereth by labor shall increase.   (xiii. 11.)

He that is slothful in his work
Is brother to him that is a great waster.   (xviii. 9.)

There can be no doubt that the people not only listened to the wise sayings, but also lived in accordance with the ethical principles communicated to them.

The Hebrew nation were of a cheerful, merry disposition, indulging in singing, playing, music, and dances. For "to sing" they had four different expressions, while "to dance" could be expressed in four or five different ways. An evident proof that these amusements were appreciated in Judea. Playing was even ascribed to Wisdom, which exclaims :

I was by him, his favorite,
Playing always before him,
Playing in his dominion,
My delights were with the sons of men.   (viii. 30, 31.)

The concourse of both sexes was not restricted. Young men and girls joined in merry dances directed by a timbrel, especially at weddings, harvest feasts, and vintage. The young men assembled in wine rooms and sang there to the sound of the tabrets. It even seems that they had regular clubs.

Family Life.

The happy family life, which, through all generations of which we possess a more exact account, was the glory and the pride of the Jews, undoubtedly also prevailed among the ancient Hebrews, when in possession of their own land. This family life was rooted in their traditions and in their religion, and we may even assert was one of the chief pillars for the preservation of the Jewish religion from entire destruction. This view appears to be expressed in the *Talmud*, where it is asserted, "Through the piety of the women Israel was redeemed from Egypt." (*Sota*, 11.) While in the outside world men were enticed to follow idols, assume strange manners and to imitate foreign costumes, in the home, at the family hearth, the good time-honored customs of the patriarchal times were retained, and the Hebrew women watched over the observance of the accustomed ceremonies. The position assigned to women was a highly honorable one, and to a certain degree independent, as appears by the entire Jewish literature and most prominently by Proverbs.

If nothing else would appear concerning the mothers of Israel in the whole Bible but the passage,

> My son, hear the instruction of thy father, and forsake
>   not the law of thy mother,
> For they shall be an ornament of grace unto thy head,
> And chains about thy neck (i. 8, 9).

it would speak volumes for the exalted position they occupied in the family. The moralist does not speak of an exceptional case, but in general of the mother, who had a large share in the education of the children and would only exercise that great influence upon them, which is so highly recommended by the quoted passage, when she possessed the moral and ethical knowledge necessary in the education of children.

We can, therefore, not be surprised when, to prove the high position of mothers in Israel, such women as Deborah and Abigail appear even as leaders of men, and the daughters of Zelophchad plead in person in defence of their rights before Moses. We may even recommend the witty Achsa to the attention of our readers, whose history is very little known, although twice related in the Bible. (Joshua xv. 16; Judges i. 15.)

Achsa, the daughter of the rich Caleb, prince of the tribe of Judah, had to marry her cousin Othniel, who, according to tradition, was a scholar, hence a poor man. Othniel, the younger son of Caleb's brother, displayed his valor in seizing Kirjath Sepher, a fortified city, and was rewarded for his exploit by the hand of Achsa. He was brave, when the hand of his fair cousin was to be won, but lost his courage when his betrothed requested him to ask for a dowry. There she herself interfered. She addressed her father in an ambiguous way, "Give me *Beracha* (both "*blessings*" and "*springs*" in Hebrew), for thou hast given me a South (*barren*) country" (referring to the poverty of her betrothed). The father granted his witty daughter a very liberal gift.

The Biblical history has very little to say about Hebrew girls, for in ancient Palestine they married at an early age, and there was very little time left for courtship with its difficulties, intrigues and romantic events, that fill modern novels, and alas! actual life. Marriage was looked upon as a holy institution ordered by divine precept.

The happy marriage of young people is beautifully conceived by our moralists:

> Rejoice with the wife of thy youth,
> Lovely as a hind, pleasant as a roe ;

> Let her embraces satisfy thee continually,
> Let her love delight thee for all time to come. (v. 18.)

Her very presence was a blessing to the household, when she fulfilled her duties:

> A woman of worth is a crown to her husband,
> A corrupt one is a rottenness in the bones. (xii. 4.)

The liberty and independence enjoyed by the women were however often misused, and quarrels in the house were the consequence.

> A contentious wife is a dripping roof. (xxvii. 15.)

> It is better to dwell in a corner of a house-top
> Than with a brawling wife in a wide house. (xxi. 9.)

> It is better to dwell in the wilderness,
> Than with a contentious, fretful woman. (xxi. 19.)

The thirty-first chapter of Proverbs (from 10–31), contains the praise and describes the properties of a good wife. This description of an ideal matron evinces the practical sense of the Israelite, which decidedly differs from the romantic, exaggerated adoration of woman, viewing her from a sentimental aspect. Herein Israelites differed from the Greeks, who in the woman only admired plastic beauty and sensuous graces.

Not that the Hebrew had no perception of the graces of woman, but in a moral code he appreciates a capable, diligent housewife, who cares for the comforts of her husband, and who watches over her household.

EDUCATION.

Among a people where marriage was regarded as a holy institution, the family hearth became a temple, with father and mother as priests; every child formed another link in the chain of love that connected them. They rejoiced in the prosperity of their children:

> My son, if thy heart be wise,
> My heart shall rejoice, even mine. (xxiii. 15.)

Both parents co-operated in the important duty of educating their children, and especially the mother laid the foundation for their future development. They were left under the care of their mothers and received from them their first instruction. Common schools were unknown. As they advanced in age, the father had to exercise his paternal authority and care. The authors of

Mishle were believers in corporal punishment, a view still maintained by some prominent modern educators.

> Chasten thy son while there is hope,
> Let not thy soul have pity for his crying. (xix. 18.)

Folly is bound in the heart of the child,
But the rod of correction shall drive it far from him. (xxii. 15.)

He that spareth his rod hateth his son,
But he that loveth him chasteneth him betimes. (xiii. 24.)

The rod and reproof give wisdom,
A child left to himself bringeth his mother to shame. (xxix. 15.)

Higher schools were established under the supervision of the prophets, to train young men to become expounders of the law, and to preserve the religion of the fathers. Such schools already existed under Samuel (I. Sam. xix. 20), and also in the time of Elijah (II. Kings ii. 5). It is also probable, that Huldah, the prophetess, dwelt in a college, as *Mishna* is translated in the R. V. and explained by some commentators. (II. Ch. xxxiv. 22.)

An important principle for education is laid down in the sentence:

> Train up the child according to his abilities,
> And when he is old he will not go astray. (xxii. 6.)

This principle is of the highest importance, and only when he regards the abilities and inclinations of the pupil can the educator expect full success to attend his efforts.

Luxury and Toilets of the Hebrew Women.

The republican simplicity which existed during the time before there were kings in Israel made room for increasing wealth, and all its advantages and defects, with the formation of the kingdom, and especially during the reigns of David and Solomon. Then arose two distinct classes, the rich and the poor, and the state of society was thereby considerably modified. During the reigns of David and Solomon the Hebrews engaged in commercial undertakings, and the products of Egypt, Arabia, and India were brought to Palestine. With the growth in wealth, luxury also increased. Not only the royal palace, but also the houses of the wealthy were built of brown cedar decorated in gold, silver, and bronze. The women rested on beds decked with coverings

---

* We take here *Derech* in the same sense as in Gen. vi. 12, "the natural inclinations."

of tapestry, surrounded by an enormous quantity of perfumes (vi. 16, 17). The fragrance of Arabia had to be imported in bulk. What abundance of boxes, vases, and bottles!

To mention some of the toilet requirements of the Hebrew ladies, we would speak of the neat cases filled with dry henna leaves, and will remark, that bunches of henna blossoms, on account of their beauty of form and their scent, were worn on the breast. (Solomon's Song i. 13.)

We also meet with *Stibium*, nothing else than antimony, which had to be transported a great distance to reach Palestine. In the Proverbs we meet with myrrh, aloe and cinnamon (vii. 17) as perfumes, all three brought from distant lands.

Did those ladies of antiquity wear many ornaments?

The moralists of *Mishle*, who wrote mostly for the middle classes, made no complaint about too much luxury of our ancestors, a decisive proof that the former republican simplicity had yet great hold among the agricultural people. Of chains, crowns, and other ornaments, our moralists only speak in connection with wisdom and teachings of parents.

The prophet Isaiah has so much the more to censure, and enumerates the following parts of dresses and garnishes: Anklets, worn as feet or ankle decorations, wherewith women made a tinkling sound in walking; little suns and moons as medals, for necklaces; ear-drops, bracelets, veils, turbans; stepchains, attached to the ankle of each foot, to compel the bearer to take short, mincing steps; girdles, smelling bottles, amulets; finger, ear, and nose rings; cloaks, money purses, mirrors of polished metal, and a few more articles about whose character we are in the dark (Is. iii. 19). We even doubt whether the eloquent prophet knew all the names of the female toilet. A moralist of *Mishle* takes occasion to speak of golden nose rings, but only in the nose of the swine.

> As a nose-ring of gold in a swine's snout,
> So is a fair woman without discernment. (xi. 22.)

COMMERCE.

The Hebrews, during the reign of the judges, were a poor, agricultural people. They received their first impulse to commercial enterprises from King Solomon. That wise king introduced commerce with the neighboring nations, and joined the Phœnicians in navigation. At that period the Babylonians and Assyrians carried on a large inland commerce, in which Palestine was included. Well constructed highroads through the desert joined Syria and Palestine with Babylon, fortified stations protected the merchants against the nomadic tribes of

Arabia, cities surrounded by walls served as resting places and magazines, and in properly situated places wells were built that provided abundant water for travelers and their beasts. These roads of the caravans may even be traced to this day. The great commercial road which crossed Galilee, from the Jacob's bridge to Capernaum, joined Ptolemais with Damascus, while another through Sebaste, the capital of Samaria, near Dothain (where Joseph was sold), passed by Beth-El to Egypt. The great caravan road to the east of the Dead Sea, along the mountains of Seir, touched Jericho, and that city became an important place for the Arabian and Egyptian trade.

Palestine, situated between Assyria, Babylonia, and Egypt, became a connecting link for these highly developed countries, and necessarily participated in the lively commerce then carried on between them and Phœnicia and Arabia. Such a commerce brought many strangers to the country, and as stated in Chronicles (ii. 2, 17), at the time of Solomon 153, 600 Gentiles resided in Jerusalem. Riches poured into the country from the mines, from taxes and tributes.

The Hebrews in the time of Solomon also joined the Phœnicians in navigation, and brought from Arabia gold and silver, ivory, apes, and peacocks.

From that time the Hebrews did not withdraw from the commerce of the world, but more or less partook in it. Our moralists in speaking of the industrious matron say :

> She is like the merchant's ships,
> She brings her food from afar   (xxxi. 14) ;

a simile which could only suggest itself in connection with a people engaged in commerce.

Uzziah, King of Judah, an excellent, prosperous monarch, attempted to imitate Solomon, and had also great ships on the sea. (Is. ii. 16.) The wealth of the country increased to such dimensions that Uzziah developed an expenditure not even known in the time of Solomon. He had a winter palace and a summer palace, and houses of ivory. (Amos iii. 15.) Luxury was exorbitant among the ruling classes. Our moralists, however, left the admonitions of these wealthy people and the merchant princes, with their vices, to the eloquent prophets, and directed their teachings merely to the petty dealers.

> It is naught, it is naught, saith the buyer,
> When he is gone his way, then he boasteth.   (xx. 14.)

> A false balance is abomination unto the Lord,
> But a just weight is his delight.   (xi. 1.)

The Principles of Ethics in the Sayings Contained in the Book of Proverbs, with an Inquiry into the Social Conditions which they Reflect.

BY GRANVILLE R. PIKE.

A people's proverbs reveal its inmost thought. They give insight into both processes and principles. This is the form naturally assumed by early and unconventional expression, before literature grows self-conscious and the spontaneous utterance of general conviction hardens into prescribed formulas. Every nation, therefore, hoary Egypt, ice-bound Finland, or China by her Yellow Sea, boasts a wealth of this minted wisdom peculiar to itself. Each holding much in common with all, the gnomic literature of every land still reveals the specific ethnic features of its birthplace, whether the æsthetic intellectualism of Greece, the military and legal bias of Rome, the vivacity of Gallic, the gravity of Teutonic, or the energy of Anglo-Saxon character.

This elliptical, sententious method of speech flourishes best, however, in the fertile fancy and contemplative habit of the Orient. Arabia, India, Persia, Judea, display their mental history and criteria of conduct in a mass of proverbial lore commensurate with the length and grandeur of their national life. Least among these ancient peoples in many ways, it is apparent from a comparison of the practical ethics abbreviated and current in these sayings that in moral elevation,—the final test of greatness,—Israel excels them all. Among her sacred writings this "wisdom" literature holds a conspicuous place. It is the subjective side of the Theocracy. The historical and prophetic portions are, in the main, objective. They set forth what God did in the process of training his people and their outward response. But these "wisdom" books show the effect of such training upon Jewish intellect and heart and conscience.

Especially does this divine influence reappear in the language and daily life and human relations in the Book of Proverbs. Its ethical principles, therefore, are grounded on God himself. This differentiates them at once, not in degree only, but in kind, from all systems based upon statute,* spiritual sovereignty of ances-

---

* Plato, *De Legibus*, lib. X. Κύρια ἕκαστα εἶναι γιγνόμενα τέκνῃ καὶ τοῖς νόμοις, ἀλλ' οὐ δή τινι φύσει.

tors,* or that no-morality of expediency against which all Hebrew literature is a protest.

In seeking the Hebrew method of determining man's complex duty, there emerge three mighty key-words as pillars which bear up the whole moral fabric. They occur grouped together as early as the third verse of the prologue, in the common version, *righteousness, judgment, equity*. צדק looks God-ward, and means a righteousness that is such by reason of its harmony with the divine character, or absolute right. משפט, resting upon the idea of judging, comes to mean the judgment reached, or the act of rendering justice, hence statute, law, that which is lawful, just. While necessarily involving social relations, it goes beyond what is simply equitable between man and man, and must conform also to the stricter demands of supreme justice. מישרים, on the contrary, is a word reflexive in its very nature. With the root-idea of straightforwardness, it signifies that which is right, *rectus*, hence undeviating rectitude of purpose, integrity. Whatever is intrinsically right, lawful in operation, and upright in motive is comprehended under these three nouns, and by them all human transactions are brought directly to the bar of God. The extent to which this conception was woven into Jewish thought is shown by the occurrence of the first of these words no less than seventy times within the small compass of this book, and each of the others appears more than a third as often. About these principles, accountability to God, mutual obligation, and personal probity, a large portion of the sayings crystallize. In them, therefore, without tedious examination of their specific applications, we find the cardinal points from which, as astronomers determine an orbit, we may trace the entire circumference where duty touches life.

Every action under an ethical system is inevitably affected by the character of its sanction. Intelligent estimate of conduct becomes possible only in response to the inquiry, to what is the ultimate appeal? Over the Delphic portals, as their profoundest precept, the Greeks inscribed KNOW THYSELF. At the opening of this collection of maxims, professedly relating mainly to worldly prudence, intellectual keenness, and business morality, the Hebrews, with deeper insight, wrote FEAR OF JEHOVAH, BEGINNING OF KNOWLEDGE. When it is remembered that by "Fear" they meant not terror, but intelligent, reverential awe, and how comprehensive also was their notion of a knowledge or wisdom

---

*Chinese Classics, Pan-King, "I think of my ancestors, who are now the spiritual sovereigns. * * * Were I to err in my government, my high sovereign would send down on me a great punishment for my crime." *Legge's Trans.*

based upon this pious attitude of mind and heart, including within it practically the whole rule of personal duty, it will readily be seen how far-reaching is the principle here announced.

It embraces alike the most ordinary and the most exalted callings and occasions. It lays a restraining hand upon the laborer, demanding that he *regard the life of his beast* (12: 10), and incites the student to the utmost strife after wisdom, that he may *understand righteousness, and judgment, and equity, yea, every good path* (2: 9).

Over this wide space between prosaic practice and highest soaring theory, consciousness of a sovereign's eye, watchful and supreme, casts a dignity for which we search other literatures in vain.

Although thou sayest, Behold, we knew not this:
Doth not he that weigheth hearts consider it?
Yea he that guardeth thy soul doth know;
And he will render to every man according to his work. (24 : 12.)

And again with even stronger emphasis,

The Under-world and Destruction are before Jehovah,
How much more then the hearts of the children of men. (15: 11.)

With so vivid a sense of the divine omniscience, a recognition of the duty of sincere worship was inevitable. Hence such sentiments as

The sacrifice of the wicked is the abomination of Jehovah;
But the prayer of the upright is his delight. (15: 8.)
Jehovah is far from the wicked;
But he heareth the prayers of the righteous. (15: 29.)

In the face of such stern discrimination between the true and the false, there is little wonder that the code of Israel found no place for that class whose breed is yet far from extinct, who would confound all moral distinctions.

He that saith unto the wicked, Thou art righteous;
Peoples shall curse him, nations shall abhor him. (24 : 24.)

Not only will he bring down upon himself the execrations of humanity, whose moral sense is outraged, but

He that justifieth the wicked, and he that condemneth the righteous,
Both of them alike are an abomination of Jehovah. (17 : 15.)

They did not, however, overlook the supplementary truth that mere lip-service or decorous performance of devotional rites was but a part, and the lesser part, of fitting worship. We seem to hear the echo of Samuel's indignant answer to Saul. (1 Sam. 15: 22), and an anticipation of Isaiah's burden (Is. 1: 11-17), in

*To do justice and judgment
Is more acceptable to Jehovah than sacrifice.* (21 : 3.)

With such impressions of God's oversight and of the sincere life which alone received his favor, it was natural that the possession of this should be reckoned chief among treasures. Consequently we are told,

*Better is little with the fear of Jehovah,
Than great treasure and trouble therewith.* (15 : 16.)

Still more apparent is the spring of honest dealing in,

*Better is a little with righteousness,
Than large revenues with injustice.* (16 : 8.)

What better antidote to the avarice which besets most hearts and all commercial peoples, and is a chief canker in our body politic to-day, than this knowledge that it is the Eternal God who strikes the final balance in the ledger!

The Israelite, conscious of his integrity, has, moreover, in this ever-present Judge a refuge from the destruction which overtakes the wicked, since whatever storms beat about him

*The name of Jehovah is a strong tower:
The righteous runneth into it and is safe.* (18 : 10.)

Hence it is that

He that walketh uprightly, walketh surely,
and *The root of the righteous shall never be moved.*

It were easy to follow the ramifications of this sense of personal accountability which underlay all Hebrew life, striking its roots deep into every department of activity, demanding that body, intellect, will, and heart render homage to Jehovah. But we address ourselves instead to tracing the influence of the nation's creed upon its social relations.

For deeds, after all, express genuine convictions. The same principles, as we soon discover, run through all this range of duties. It is still Jehovah who *guards the paths of judgment.* (2 : 8.)

In the field of general ethics, worthy to stand at the head of all precepts, is this : *Say not, I will do so to him as he hath done to me : I will render to the man according to his work.* (24: 29.) This surpasses that ancient maxim of Confucius, What ye would not that men should do to you, that do ye not to them, inasmuch as the Chinese injunction is merely negative, forbidding only the initiative in evil, while the Jew is enjoined to suffer injury in patience and trust in him who saith, Vengeance is mine, I will repay. If revenge is so strongly prohibited, much more the more obvious sins against life and liberty. The reason urged for not joining the robber bands, described 1: 10–19, is that *they make haste to shed blood.* Among the six things hated of Jehovah (6: 16-19) are *hands that shed innocent blood*, and a malicious person who causeth the upright to err, *shall fall into his own pit.* Property rights are guarded by warnings against theft, robbery, monopoly, cheating. Especially is stress laid upon fair dealing between man and man, and the strictest honesty required :

A just balance and scales are Jehovah's,
All the weights of the bag are his work. (16 : 11.)

What a revolution must be wrought in the commercial morality of any modern people, in order to render universally acceptable such a sentiment as,

Balances of deceit are the abomination of Jehovah;
But a just weight is his delight!

Because *lying lips are the abomination of Jehovah*, the Hebrew theory of right tolerated no slander; and a false witness was *a maul, and a sword, and a sharp arrow.* On the other hand the cultivation of a charitable disposition was regarded as of prime importance. *If thine enemy be hungry, give him bread to eat; and if he be thirsty, give him water to drink.*

* * * * *Jehovah shall reward thee.* (25 : 21.) Particularly, there was required kindness to the poor, who were counted wards of the Almighty; *He that oppresseth the poor reproacheth his Maker; But he that hath mercy on the needy honoreth him.* (14 : 31.) *The* RIGHTEOUS *taketh knowledge of the cause of the poor.* (29 : 7.)

It is obvious that these and many similar passages teach a philanthropy as genuine and, because founded directly upon God, more enduring than the boasted Altruism at present so fashionable in certain circles. Perhaps, however, no better gauge of a people's morals can be found than the relative position of the family. When lax views concerning that prevail, the whole social fabric is unsound. Israel is conspicuous in history for the sacredness with which she invested the marriage relation : *Whoso findeth a wife, findeth a good thing, and obtaineth favor of Jehovah.* (18 : 22.) No warnings are more frequent or solemn than those against matrimonial infidelity. Parental responsibilities, and the reciprocal duties of children are emphasized repeatedly, and we need not stop to illustrate them, for the sufficient reason that these maxims are already in everybody's mouth.

Exploring the still subtler sources of conduct as manifested by the individual, we trace these also to this common fountain of all the rest. *He who walketh in his integrity, feareth the Lord.* (14 : 2.)

How thoroughly the conviction that, to those on God's side, all things work together for good, was imbedded in Jewish thought, may be seen in such profound conceptions as, *the wicked is a ransom for the righteous;*

And the treacherous cometh in the room of the upright (21 : 18), or, *The wealth of the sinner is laid up for the righteous.* (13: 22). That the prevalence of such sentiments was not a substitute for personal exertion, but an incentive to it, even a cursory examination makes abundantly evident. Feeling themselves God-kept, they felt more than selfish interest in keeping themselves. It was a religious duty as well.

Since the primal command, "In the sweat of thy face shalt thou eat bread," a fundamental element of this self-conservation is *industry*. It emulates, in Proverbs, the God-given instinct of the ant, which *Provideth her food in the summer.* (6 : 8.) It preserves from the fate of the slothful, who *shall come under tribute.* (12 : 24.) It is a defence against the *strong man armed* of Poverty (24 : 34), and raises the diligent to the fellowship of kings (22 : 29). Closely allied, too, with zeal in getting, is economy in use, and frugality in spending ; He that *loveth wine and oil shall not be rich.* (21 : 17.)

The educational scheme of the Hebrews contemplated cultivation of the intellect, but not alone nor as an end in itself. The spiritual was to be cultivated through the intellect. This thought sounds like the ever-recurring keynote of a symphony throughout Proverbs. Consequently, wherever we find a suggestion of mental culture, almost invariably it is mentioned as simply the gateway to moral enlightenment. Thus the outcome of seeking *knowledge as silver* (2: 4), is that thou shalt *understand the fear of the Lord, and find the knowledge of God.* As might be expected from such fundamental principles, we find great emphasis put upon development of the moral nature: *Keep thy heart with all diligence; For out of it are the issues of life.* (16 : 19.) The impossibility of such keeping, without practicing the elementary virtue of self-restraint, is acknowledged in such sentiments as: Whosoever is deceived by wine is not wise (20: 1); He that curbs his own spirit excels the military conqueror (16: 32); and he that is beguiled by the blandishments of the courtesan is *void of understanding* (7 : 7). Guided by such principles, and watchful in their application,

*The path of the righteous is as the dawning light,
That shineth more and more unto the perfect day.* (4 : 18.)

As the traveler, pausing on a country's border, lingers a little to call before him its varied features and diverse scenes, and blend them all into a single characteristic picture which he may carry with him while hastening on to other lands, so may we profitably turn now a short backward glance upon the territory thus rapidly traversed, while we inquire what are the social conditions of the region of our sojourn. It is no easy life to portray upon a single canvass. There have passed before us the hunter and the husbandman ; the soldier and the statesman ; the man of high estate and the brother of low degree. We have passed among the lowing herds, the ripening vintage, and the busy mart, through mirthful and through serious hours. But through them all the Hebrew has been grave and earnest, like Isaac in the fields at eventide. Life, with him, is a reality, with an impartial Judge to mark his good or ill. Consequently these Proverbs which show us the innermost thought, the feelings, reasonings, and moral impulses of Hebrew society, show us at the same time a people whom it is impossible not to respect. Their close communion with Jehovah and constant life in his sight elevated the mind and disciplined the judgment of the whole people. Hence the phenomenon, without a parallel, of a nation in which such sentiments and sayings could become current coin. To speak, in a single word, the volume to which this exhibit of Israel's social condition through her Proverbs invites, the social condition of the originators may fairly be assumed to be in many points akin to that of a nation largely moulded by these sayings—Scotland.

Printed by Libri Plureos GmbH in Hamburg, Germany